fast fun & easy

NEEDLE FELTING

**8 Techniques & Projects
—Creative Results in Minutes**

Lynne Farris

C&T PUBLISHING

Text © 2006 Lynne Farris

Artwork ©2006 C&T Publishing, Inc.

Publisher: Amy Marson

Editorial Director: Gailen Runge

Acquisitions Editor: Jan Grigsby

Editor: Gailen Runge

Technical Editors: Nanette S. Zeller, Elin Thomas

Copyeditor and Proofreader: Wordfirm Inc

Design Director/Book Designer: Kristy K. Zacharias

Illustrator: Tim Manibusan

Production Assistant: Zinnia Heinzmann

Photography by C&T Publishing, Inc. unless otherwise noted

Published by C&T Publishing, Inc., P.O. Box 1456, Lafayette, CA, 94549

Library of Congress Cataloging-in-Publication Data

Farris, Lynne
    Fast, fun & easy needle felting : 8 techniques & projects - creative results in minutes! / Lynne Farris.
      p. cm.
    ISBN-13: 978-1-57120-397-7 (paper trade : alk. paper)
    ISBN-10: 1-57120-397-4 (paper trade : alk. paper)
    1. Felt work. 2. Felting. I. Title. II. Title: Fast, fun and easy needle felting.

    TT849.5.F37 2006
    746'.0463—dc22

    2006011481

Printed in China

10 9 8 7 6 5 4 3 2 1

Acknowledgments

Special thanks to Carol Duvall for her enthusiasm and generosity in letting me share my love of needle felting on several occasions with her wonderful HGTV audience.

Thanks to Jack and Julie Pierce of Atlanta Sewing Center for their ongoing support of my creativity and to the wonderful people at Babylock who provided the fabulous embellisher machine. Thanks to Weeks Dye Works, National Nonwovens, and Colonial Needle for generous donations of wool, fibers, and tools.

Thanks and smiles to my friends the Artgirlz, Alison and Tracy Stillwell, who shared their idea for the felted bracelet and whose creative collaboration inspires us all.

Special thanks to Gabrielle Kinge for unbridled enthusiasm for all our creative projects, and to Lambert Greene for getting them all to FedEx before they lock the doors at night.

Special thanks to my friends at C&T Publishing, Jan Grigsby, Gailen Runge, Amy Marson, and their entire team of creative professionals for giving me this wonderful opportunity and for making it come together with lightning speed.

Finally, thanks to you for your interest in needle felting. Enjoy!

Lynne Farris

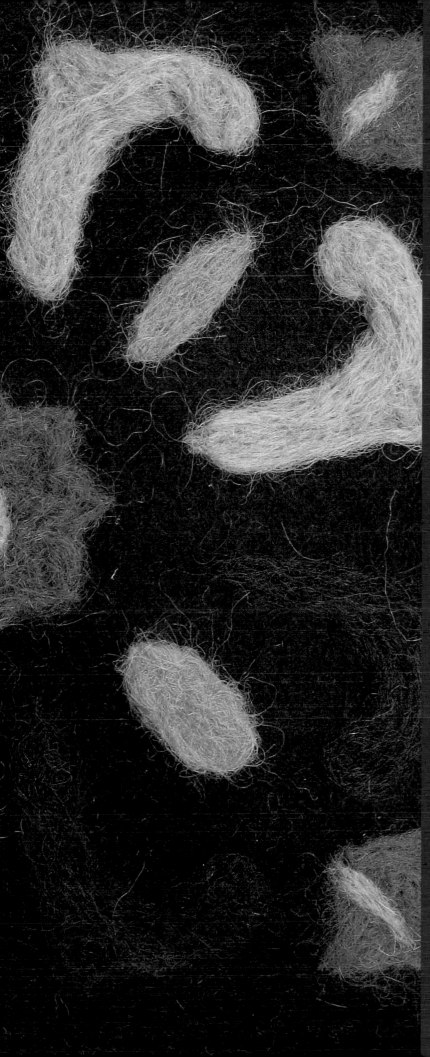

Contents

Introduction

I've been creating with fabric my whole life. It started when my grandmother helped me make clothes for my little dolls. As a young adult, I lucked into the ultimate creative dream job when I worked for a while at a toy company, designing stuffed animals (once again, playing with dolls!). My fascination with all things fabric led me to continue creating bigger and wackier stuff with fabric. This continued right up to the point at which I knew I had gone too far: I actually agreed to transform a golf cart into a whale by covering it with foam and fabric. I'll spare you the details, but once I recovered from that little adventure, I resolved to confine my creative fabric projects to a more "manageable" scale.

Many years ago I attended a traditional felting workshop led by a local artist. I loved the fiber, the fabulous colors, and the felt itself, but found dealing with all the soapy water and mess and the time involved to be quite cumbersome. What I really wanted was something more direct, like painting, but involving fabric and providing instant gratification. As luck would have it, I saw a needle felting demonstration while attending a trade show several years later and was immediately hooked! It's the perfect medium for me. There's all the great fabric-related stuff you can create with; the results are spectacular; and it's truly fast, fun, and easy!

I'm delighted to introduce you to this fascinating and versatile medium. Prepare to be smitten, and have fun felting!

Lynne Farris

all the basics

You can needle felt quite successfully the first time you try it. This book is all about getting started.

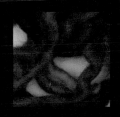
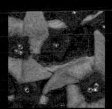
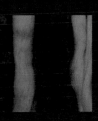

Felting Basics

a few felt facts

Felting is an ancient method of creating a nonwoven fabric by entangling fibers so that they become permanently joined. Historically, felt has been an important fabric in many cultures, used for making clothing, shoes and boots, costumes and ritual masks, rugs, bedding, and furniture. In fact some nomadic families in Mongolia live in round, tent-like dwellings called "yurts" constructed almost entirely from thick felt. It is thought that ancient nomadic tribesmen may have discovered felt somewhat accidentally when they placed layers of wool fleece under their saddles for extra comfort. The agitation of the saddle against the fleece as they rode through the desert probably caused the fleece to entangle, or to become felted.

wet felting

Some felting methods require the wool fibers to be wet with a soapy solution and then agitated for a period of time to cause the fibers to felt. Actually, if you have ever tossed your favorite wool sweater in the washing machine only to have it turn out shrunk, matted, and much thicker, you have experienced wet felting yourself.

needle felting

Dry felting or needle felting is adapted from commercial felt manufacturers who use giant machinery with literally thousands of needles to create huge rolls of needle-punched felt fabric. In this method burred needles are inserted through layers of wool or synthetic fibers. The small burrs on the needles catch onto the fibers, which are then pulled through as the needles move up and down, so that the fibers become "mechanically entangled." Fiber artists have literally taken these same industrial burred needles into their own hands and come up with all kinds of techniques for creating and embellishing fabric by hand.

getting started

Here's some good news: absolutely no previous experience or skill is required. You can needle felt quite successfully the first time you try it. This book is all about getting started. The projects are designed to familiarize you with the basic techniques so that you can put your own creative felting ideas into action. As you will see, even though needle felting comes from ancient traditions, it is a versatile medium, perfect for contemporary designer looks.

a couple of things you should know

Hazardous Tools

Felting needles are VERY sharp!

It's important to keep the business end of the needle away from your fingers, even when you have to hold onto your project. Some people like to use finger guards on the hand that's not holding the needle. You're going to be piercing your project repeatedly, and it's easy to get carried away and forget to watch what you're doing. (A side benefit of all that "repeated piercing" is that you'll find needle felting to be a great tool for anger management.) At any rate, be careful and pay attention to what you're doing. And don't even *think* about working in your lap while watching TV!

Hazardous Conditions

The very fact that you're going to be piercing your project repeatedly implies repetitive motion—ergo, ergonomics! It's important to sit comfortably at a work surface that is the proper height so that your back is straight and you can support your elbow, forearm, and wrist on the table. You might find it comfortable to rest your wrist on the edge of a foam pad while working.

Tools and Materials

what you'll need

One of the most enjoyable aspects of embarking on a new creative pursuit is the hunting and gathering phase, you know, acquisition therapy, where you get to go out and collect all the stuff! You'll find some great sources for cool stuff in the resource guide, and there are all kinds of delightful and unusual needle felting goodies available on the Internet. As the popularity of needle felting continues to explode, I'm sure there will be even more great stuff. But this list will certainly get you equipped with the basics and poised to create.

materials

Fabric: For the most part, you will be working on some sort of base fabric such as wool felt, felted woven wool, or knitted wool (think recycled sweater).

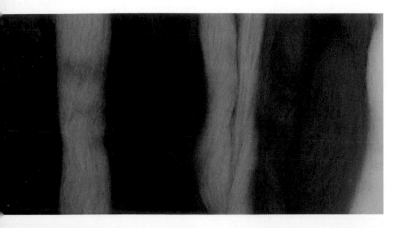

Wool roving: Wool fiber that has been dyed and carded so that the fibers are smooth and aligned. It is also sometimes called sliver. Available in oodles of delicious colors. You can use it to embellish fabric or start from scratch and create your own fabric from layers of roving.

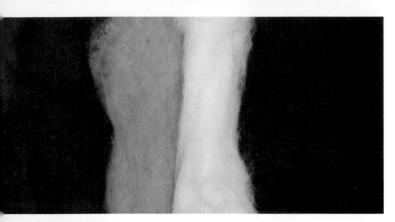

Wool fleece: Wool fiber that has not been carded—it's quite fluffy and looks more like batting. It can be used in pretty much the same way as roving; it just doesn't look quite as smooth. Great for dimensional needle felting because it entangles quite readily.

Yarn: You can use up your yarn scraps to felt onto a project or to draw outlines around your designs, coloring book style.

Embellishments: Needle felting is the perfect surface for embellishing with beads, buttons, charms, embroidery, trims, cords, and ribbons, and any other little snippets you have in your stash. As with any creative effort, too much is never quite enough!

tools

Felting needle: A pointed metal needle, about 3½″ to 4″ long, triangular on the pointed end, with nicks or burrs cut at several intervals near the end. You can work with a single needle for outlines or detail work or use several together for larger areas. There are actually several different styles and types of needles, but for me, a basic 36-gauge needle worked just fine for all the projects in this book.

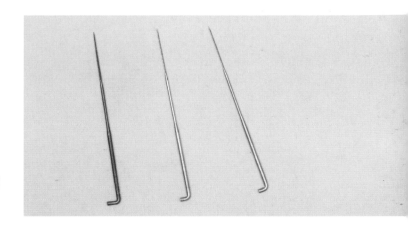

Foam pad: This is the surface you will work on as you poke and pierce the fibers and fabric repeatedly. It will protect your work table as well as your needles. Ideally, the pad should be about 1½″ to 2″ thick and fairly dense. It should also be large enough so that you don't have to constantly lift up your project and move it around.

Multineedle tool: Used to hold several needles at once. Several versions that give you options for quickly covering large areas are available.

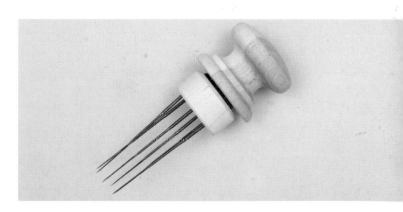

Scissors: Good sharp, pointed scissors are essential to a successful project.

Rotary cutter, gridded cutting mat, and clear straight-edge ruler: These are essential for trimming up edges and cutting felt. You might even like to use a pinking-edged rotary blade for some projects.

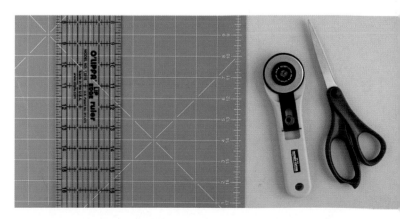

Steam iron and press cloth: You will want to steam some areas of your projects to smooth the wool fabric, to further felt the fibers, or to reduce the visibility of holes left by the needles.

Markers: I like to use air soluble markers or chalk markers, depending on the color of fabric I'm working on. Avoid ink or permanent markers.

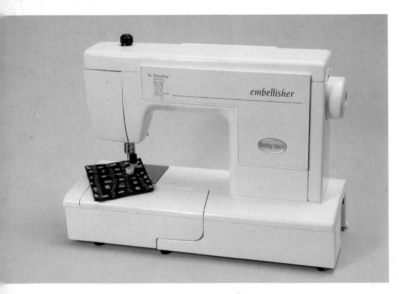

Embellisher machine: OK, it's not exactly basic but, trust me, once you've been bitten by the needle felting bug, you're going to want one. Babylock's embellisher machine (*see Resources*) looks a lot like a sewing machine, but it can hold up to seven needles, and it makes quick work of needle felting. Oh, so fast!!! And oh, so cool!

felting as surface embellishment

NEEDLE FELTED MINI-SEASCAPE

One of the easiest ways to get started needle felting is to apply roving to an existing fabric surface to create an allover pattern, an abstract design, or even a simple picture.

What You'll Need

- [ ] 12″ × 12″ square ivory wool or wool felt for background (will be trimmed to 5″ × 5″ after washing)
- [ ] Colored wool roving in your favorite palette for seascape
- [ ] Brown and green felted wool yarn scraps
- [ ] 5″ × 5″ square tulle or nylon veiling
- [ ] Baking soda
- [ ] Markers, air soluble or chalk, and permanent
- [ ] Felting needle
- [ ] Foam pad
- [ ] Seed and bugle beads
- [ ] Beading needle and threads
- [ ] Optional: mat and/or frame

Your finished piece can be matted and framed to use as a decorative accent for your favorite room, as an embellishment for a journal cover or pillow, or as a pin to adorn a handbag or hat.

By felting colorful wool roving fibers onto a solid wool background, you can create tiny jewel-like pictures of seascapes, landscapes, cityscapes, and still life images. For inspiration, you can look at travel posters or your own vacation photos.

How-Tos
preparing fabric

1. To prepare the background fabric, choose a solid or heather wool or wool felt. Wash in the washing machine with ½ cup of baking soda using hot water, and dry on high temperature to "felt" the fibers. The fabric will shrink considerably, so start with a larger piece than you need to have. Steam press fabric to flatten.

2. Using a permanent marker, copy pattern template (page 45) onto tulle. Then, center tulle on background fabric, pin in place, and trace tulle pattern with air soluble or chalk marker. Remove tulle from background, and retrace to define lines, if necessary. Or sketch your own design on paper, and transfer it to the background fabric with tulle.

easy!

Look through children's coloring books for simple line drawings of birds, butterflies, flowers, and landscapes to use as inspiration for new felting projects.

beginning to felt

1. Place background fabric onto foam pad. Arrange roving onto the background in the general shape of the sky, and then use the felting needle to pierce the surface repeatedly so that roving fibers become embedded into background fabric.

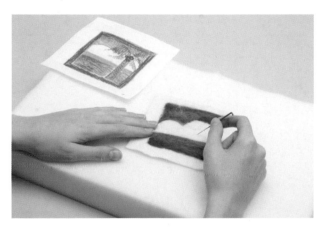

2. Add more roving to create cloud shapes and water, and then add smaller details such as the sun and the thin sandbar so that the seascape begins to take shape.

3. To make the palm tree, use a length of brown felted wool yarn for the trunk. Position yarn on felted background, and needle felt in place along edges, carefully maintaining the dimensional quality of the thick yarn.

4. Create the palm fronds by splitting a piece of green felted wool yarn at one end, leaving the other end intact. Needle felt in place, joining intact end of yarn to trunk and leaving split fibers free for palm fronds.

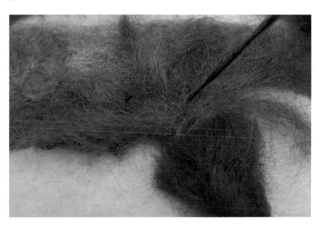

5. Use a longer piece of brown wool yarn to needle felt a dimensional frame around outer edges of picture. Begin and end at base of palm tree, overlapping ends and needle felting to secure.

easy!

If you are planning on matting and framing your masterpiece, you can start with a precut mat and format your project to fit snugly in the frame.

finishing touches

Using completed project photo as a guide, embellish sun and sea with miniature seed beads and bugle beads. The bugle beads on the water will look like reflections of the sun. Add novelty beads at base of palm fronds to simulate coconuts.

To finish, if completed project is to be used as an appliqué on a pillow or handbag, trim background fabric edges close to yarn frame. Attach to surface by carefully sewing background with matching or invisible thread and hiding stitches under yarn frame.

fun!

Simple dots and stripes can look fresh and contemporary when translated through the medium of needle felting—check out our needle felted recycled sweater pillow (B in Variations).

fast!

Add a pin back to a minidesign, and pin it onto a hat, handbag, or lapel.

Variations

A. You can make a three-dimensional grove of shady trees dappled with sunlight. Begin by needle felting layers of horizontal strips of roving to simulate ground and horizon, and then add vertical lengths of felted wool yarn for the tree trunks. Finish by overlaying green and yellow-green horizontal roving to simulate foliage on the trees.

B. How about needle felting colorful patterns directly onto a recycled wool sweater pillow? Start by washing sweater in hot water with ½ cup of baking soda and drying on high heat. Cut front and back, and sew together as a pillow cover for a premade pillow form. Place onto pillow, and hand sew closed. Create stripes and dots of colored roving, and needle felt into place directly onto pillow surface.

C. Needle felt a brightly colored pattern onto a strip of felt, and then glue it onto the cover of a handmade journal for a thoughtful one-of-a-kind hostess gift.

D. Use small scraps of felt and bits of roving to create abstract minidesigns. You can attach them to note cards for a great gift or attach pin backs and wear them on a hat, handbag, or lapel.

A B

C D

mosaic appliqué

NEEDLE FELTED MOSAIC JOURNAL COVER

You can dress up a plain fabric-covered journal to create this spectacular personal journal, sure to inspire regular visits from the muse.

What You'll Need

- [ ] 4″ × 6″ rectangle wool felt for background
- [ ] 4½″ × 6½″ rectangle wool felt for border
- [ ] 5½″ × 7½″ rectangle contrasting wool felt for mat
- [ ] Wool felt scraps in various colors to cut up for leaves, berries, and flowers (see color key on page 45)
- [ ] Small bits of dyed wool roving or fleece
- [ ] 1 sheet card stock paper

- [ ] Marker, air soluble or chalk
- [ ] Felting needle
- [ ] Foam pad
- [ ] 6″ × 8″ fabric-covered journal
- [ ] Rotary cutter, ruler, and mat
- [ ] 1 sheet Supertape double-sided adhesive, 8½″ × 11″ (ThermoWeb, *see Resources*)
- [ ] Optional: multineedle tool or embellisher machine

One of my favorite needle felting techniques is mosaic appliqué, which involves cutting small shapes from felt or other wooly fabric, arranging them onto a contrasting background fabric, and needle felting the layers together to form an interesting abstract composition or pictorial design. The finished piece can be used to embellish a journal cover, as shown; added to a plain pillow, handbag, or jacket to create a one of-a-kind designer look; or used as an eye-catching piece of wall art to add personal style to your home.

fast!

Using a multineedle tool or embellisher machine makes the felting process go faster.

How-Tos
preparing design

1. Photocopy pattern template (page 45) onto card stock paper. Or sketch your own design on paper, and make a card stock copy.

2. Cut up the card stock pattern into areas of color, and use marker to trace pattern piece outlines onto felt scraps.

3. Cut out felt pieces.

easy!

Create smaller versions of your designs, and needle felt onto small strips of wool felt to use as bookmarks.

beginning to felt

1. Cover background fabric with press cloth, and press to remove any wrinkles or folds.

2. Place background fabric onto foam pad. Using pattern template as a guide, arrange larger felt pieces, such as leaves, stem, and flowers, onto the background. With a felting needle, multineedle tool, or embellisher machine, pierce surface repeatedly until felt pieces become embedded into background fabric.

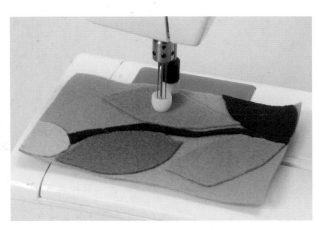

3. Add smaller pieces, such as veins in leaves and flower centers, and needle felt into place until the layers become embedded and secure. Use small bits of roving to help felt pieces together or to add texture and shading.

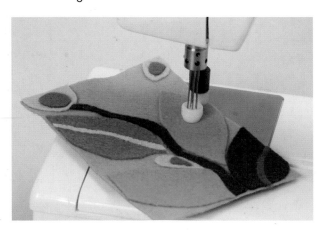

4. When felting is complete, you may notice that the edges of your appliqué have become slightly distorted. Use a rotary cutter and ruler to trim off distorted edges.

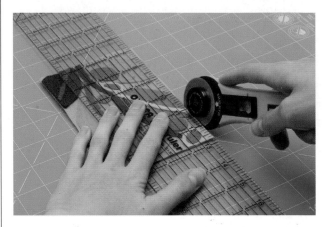

5. Place felted mosaic background on border fabric, and needle felt all over to attach layers. With rotary cutter and ruler, trim border to ¼˝ around all sides.

finishing touches

To finish, follow manufacturer's instructions for applying double-sided adhesive to wrong side of border fabric. Peel away backing paper, and adhere bordered mosaic, centered, on mat fabric. Apply double-sided adhesive to wrong side of mat, trimming edges to ensure that adhesive covers entire surface. Peel away backing paper, and adhere matted mosaic to front of journal.

fun!

Make a mosaic appliqué flower, and attach a pin back so you can perk up a jacket lapel or hat brim with a bright spot of color.

Variations

A. Instead of making flower and leaf shapes, you can re-create interesting mosaic tile patterns by cutting felt scraps into ½″ squares and strips. Place background fabric on foam pad, and arrange felt pieces on background. Leave small gaps between tiles so that background fabric shows through. Pierce each felt piece a few times with a felting needle to hold in place. Remove foam pad carefully to avoid disturbing design. Use an embellisher machine to felt layers together.

B. Make really cool wall art. Cut out felt shapes or letters, and needle felt onto contrasting squares. Then needle felt those squares onto artist's stretchers covered with black felt. Embellish with yarn and felt fringe if desired.

C. Make three-dimensional appliqué flowers. Cut out flower shapes or felt fringe. Create flower centers from roving, and needle felt flowers onto background fabric, leaving petals free.

creating felt fabric
from roving

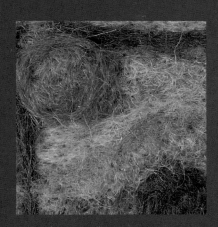

CHUNKY, NEEDLE FELTED WAFERS

Perfect for a special set of notes, or add a pin back and a few beads, and you've got jewels!

What You'll Need

- Small pieces of wool roving or fleece in several related colors for background
- Bits of wool roving in several colors that contrast with background colors
- Multicolored felted wool trimmings and wool yarn scraps from previous projects
- Felting needle
- Foam pad
- 1 sheet Supertape double-sided adhesive, 8½″ × 11″ (ThermoWeb, see *Resources*)
- Rotary cutter, ruler, and mat
- Optional: multineedle tool or embellisher machine
- Optional: tulle
- Optional: beads, beading needle, and threads

The real magic of needle felting is that you can actually design and create your own fabric from roving or batting. It's fun to let the fiber take you where it wants to go; add wisps of roving, twirled around a finger, then attach onto the surface to create a circle or a dot, or use bits of leftover yarn and even snippets and trimmings of felt from previous projects. The cards and pin featured here use this technique to great advantage.

M-m-m-m, these wafers sound delicious! First you have the fun of creating these tasty little needle felted morsels. Then you get to enjoy seeing someone's face light up when you give them as a gift!

How Tos
preparing design

The good news is that there are no rules or templates for making the wafers. Your own personal sense of color and design will reveal itself as you allow yourself to play with color, shape, and texture. You can be very specific about matching colors to a favorite scarf or jacket, or you can throw caution to the wind and experiment with whatever scraps of yarn, fiber, and felt are in your stash from previous projects.

However you decide to approach the project, rest assured that you can continue layering and felting until you like it or at the very least, you can slice it up and use the parts to embellish the next one. In any event, let yourself enjoy hanging out with the unknown on this project, and you will be richly rewarded.

beginning to felt

1. Start by stacking several layers of roving so that the fibers in one layer run perpendicular to the previous layer. Your stack will be rather fluffy at first.

fast!

When starting to create your fabric, add a layer of tulle between layers of roving to add stability.

2. Begin piercing repeatedly with felting needle, multineedle tool, or embellisher until the fibers become entangled. The more the fibers are pierced, the denser the fabric will become.

3. Fold the soft-felted piece in half, and continue needle felting, creating a thicker and smaller fiber wafer.

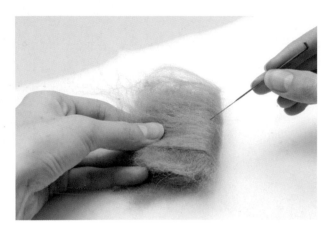

4. Add wisps of contrasting roving on top, and needle felt into a plaid or striped pattern. Twirl a bit of roving around your fingertip, and felt a circle pattern.

5. Arrange small bits of multicolored felt trimmings and yarn scraps, and needle felt, adding roving as necessary to hold the pieces in place.

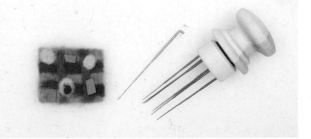

fun!

Simple dots and stripes can look fresh and contemporary when translated through the medium of needle felting. For inspiration, think of tic-tac-toe, checkerboard, or allover polka-dot patterns.

finishing touches

To finish, trim off distorted edges using a rotary cutter and ruler. (Save trimmings for another project.) Add beads, if desired.

To attach to cards, apply extra-strong double-sided adhesive to back side of felt wafer. Peel away backing paper, and then center and attach to purchased cards.

fun!

Instead of a square, cut your felt into a circle. Add dots of roving all over, needle felt onto the surface, and then sew on some shiny beads in the centers of the dots.

Variation

Create several wafers, and adhere onto a coordinating mat in a horizontal row. Place in a simple frame, and you're an instant artiste!

dimensional
felt sculpting

BLOOMIN' HATBAND ACCENT

In a matter of just a few minutes you can transform an ordinary purchased hat into a fabulous fashion statement by adding a felted fantasy flower accent.

What You'll Need

- [ ] Wool roving in light and dark shades of purple for flower
- [ ] Small bit of yellow wool roving for flower center
- [ ] 1″ × 5″ rectangle red wool felt, cut into ⅛″ fringe
- [ ] 4″ × 5″ green felted wool for leaves
- [ ] Bits of yarn for leaf veins
- [ ] Felting needle
- [ ] Foam pad
- [ ] Rotary cutter, ruler, and mat
- [ ] Sewing needle and coordinating thread

The fibers used in making felt are dimensional by nature in that they are buoyant and thick. Furthermore, you can easily join one piece to another almost seamlessly simply by piercing repeatedly with the felting needle so that the fibers from one piece become entangled with the fibers from the other.

How Tos
preparing design

You'll probably start with a particular color in mind to match your hat, then add a layer of roving in a tint (a lighter shade) of that same color for contrast when felting your swirly flower shape. Then you'll want a contrasting color with some intensity for the fringe that will serve as a backdrop for your flower center and a light yellow or green spot for the flower center to draw the eye in as a focal point. The leaves and band should coordinate with the hat, meaning that their intensity, whether bright or muted, should be similar to that of the hat.

beginning to felt

1. Arrange two layers of purple roving so that the fibers in one layer run perpendicular and are contrasting in color to the previous layer. The stack should be about 6″ × 9″ and will be rather fluffy at first.

2. Begin piercing repeatedly with your felting needle until the fibers become lightly entangled.

3. Fold the soft-felted piece in thirds lengthwise to create a long rectangle about 2″ × 9″. Needle felt to secure the folded layers. With a rotary cutter and

ruler, trim one long edge, revealing the dark and light layers.

4. Begin rolling from one short end of felted roving to create a cylinder shape approximately 2″ in diameter with a swirl along the cut edge.

5. Tuck the loose end of roving to the underside of the swirl, and needle felt to join fibers together. Continue needle felting around outside of ball to compact and secure the layers.

6. Attach the yellow roving to the center of the swirl, and needle felt in place to create the flower center.

7. Arrange the red fringe around the outer edge of flower, and needle felt in place.

8. Cut out 2 green leaf shapes from felted wool, and needle felt yarn through leaf centers for veins.

9. Needle felt leaves onto back of flower.

fun!

Embellish your flower centers with colorful seed beads to add sparkle.

finishing touches

Use a needle and thread to attach flower to hatband.

Variations

A. Create your own felt, and cut out thick felt petals and leaves. Felt in place, and glue onto the top of a fabric-covered keepsake box.

B. Create a really cool monogram wall piece. Cut out chunky thick felt letters, arrange onto a frame stretched with felt and embellish with bits of yarn, roving, and a funky fringe flower.

A

B

millefiori buttons and beads

FELTED BEAD BRACELET

Create this colorful bracelet tonight, and wear it tomorrow. It's so quick and versatile, you will want to make lots of them with oodles of variations.

What You'll Need

- ☐ Wool felt in several colors
- ☐ Wool roving in coordinating colors
- ☐ Small scraps of yarn in coordinating colors
- ☐ 1 yard waxed linen thread
- ☐ ¾″ button
- ☐ 12–15 small glass beads for button loop
- ☐ Felting needle
- ☐ Foam pad
- ☐ Beading needle
- ☐ Rotary cutter, ruler, and mat
- ☐ Sharp scissors

This great project idea from artists Alison and Tracy Stillwell showcases millefiori and needle felted bead-making techniques. You could also use these same techniques on a much larger scale for sculpting and dimensional felting work, but here's just a mini-sampler to whet your felt bead-making appetite.

How-Tos
preparing design

There are no rules or patterns for this project, so you can really have fun deciding on color schemes and materials for these bracelets. You can match a special outfit, or simply use all your favorite colors for a colorful confetti look. Experiment with coordinating the felted beads and felt squares, or you might try a stylish black-and-white scheme with one red felted millefiori bead to add a touch of drama to your soft jewelry. Embellish with charms, buttons, and beads as you wish, to give a distinctive look to each new creation.

fun!

Make millefiori beads, and glue them to button backs. Use these stylish art-to-wear replacement buttons on a favorite jacket.

beginning to felt

Millefiori Beads

1. Cut 2 strips ¾″ × 8″ of contrasting wool felt.

2. Starting at one short end, roll the 2 layers tightly together. Trim the sides as necessary to create even edges.

3. Carefully needle felt all around the rolled layers, piercing from the outside toward the center and being certain to secure outside ends of felt strips. Some slight shifting of the layers may occur during the felting process. If so, use sharp scissors to even up the layers.

Felted Beads

1. Start with a small clump of roving or batting about 2″ in diameter. Roll lightly between palms to shape loosely into a ball.

2. Place on foam pad, and carefully pierce with a felting needle around all sides to compact and shape the roving into a round bead.

3. As the bead becomes more compact, insert felting needle, and pierce repeatedly without removing point of needle, firming up inside of bead. Reposition needle, and repeat this process from several directions.

4. Once your bead is fairly firm, you can embellish it by adding small bits of coordinating roving or yarn to the outside, needle felting them in place as desired. Create 4 felted beads.

finishing touches

1. Using a rotary cutter and ruler, cut ½″-wide felt strips in several colors, then cut strips into ½″ squares. Depending on the thickness of your felt and size of your beads, you will need approximately 80 squares ½″ × ½″ to complete the 8″ bracelet shown.

2. To assemble the bracelet, thread beading needle, double-stranded, with 1 yard of waxed linen thread. Attach button to the thread, and knot on back side to secure.

3. Begin threading felt squares onto bracelet in pairs, arranging pairs in a pleasing sequence of colors. Continue threading felt squares until 11 pairs are attached, and then add a felted bead.

fun!

Add a funky charm to your bracelet by threading one on between felt shapes.

4. Thread 9 more pairs of felt squares, and then add a felted bead, your millefiori bead, and another felted bead. Continue with 9 more pairs of squares, a felted bead, and finish up with 11 pairs of squares.

9 felt squares, felted bead, millefiori bead
(Note: To match the bracelet exactly,
use pairs of same-color felt squares.)

easy!

Make a bracelet completely out of needle felted beads, no felt squares.

5. Thread on the small glass beads, and shape into a loop. Test to be certain that the loop fits over the plastic button; add more glass beads if necessary.

6. Guide your needle back through the entire sequence of felt squares, millefiori button, and beads in reverse order. End by threading the needle through the holes of the button. Loop needle and thread to the back of the button, and tie off securely with several knots. Trim thread ends.

fast!

Use glass beads between each felt shape, and reduce the number of felt pieces needed by ½.

creating designs
with stencils

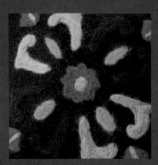

MINI FLANGE PILLOW

This tiny pillow will add the perfect touch of color and texture to brighten up a side chair; you can create a coordinated trio to heighten the impact.

What You'll Need

- [ ] 8″ × 8″ square wool felt in a dark color for background
- [ ] 1 wool felt square 10″ × 10″ for pillow front
- [ ] 2 wool felt rectangles 7″ × 10″ for pillow back
- [ ] Wool roving in choice of colors
- [ ] Premade 7″ pillow form (Lynne Farris Designs, see Resources)
- [ ] 6″ stencil (Plaid Simply Stencils, see Resources)
- [ ] Foam pad
- [ ] Felting needle
- [ ] Tape, masking or artist
- [ ] Rotary cutter, ruler, and mat
- [ ] Sewing machine and coordinating thread

Another great technique to get you started with needle felting is using a stencil to guide you as you work. This little minipillow features a stylized pattern reminiscent of antique ceramic tiles, but with updated style and palette.

How-Tos
preparing design

For best results select a simple stencil design with large open areas.

beginning to felt

1. Arrange background fabric onto foam pad, and center stencil on top. Use tape to secure stencil to background.

2. Begin by applying a small amount of colored roving into an open area of the stencil; with a felting needle pierce repeatedly around the outer edges to define the shape. Continue needle felting until area is filled in and roving has become compacted. For longer shapes, grasp roving between thumb and forefinger, and hold taut, guiding roving into shape as you work. Continue until all open areas are filled.

3. Pull stencil carefully away from background, leaving one side taped. Inspect edges of shapes, and neaten as necessary.

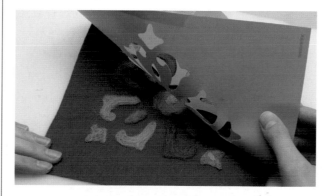

4. Remove stencil when needle felting is complete. Then gently and carefully pull felted piece up from foam pad.

5. Trim with a rotary cutter and ruler to even up any distorted edges.

finishing touches

1. Center felted background onto 10″ × 10″ pillow front, pin in place, and sew around background ¼″ from edge.

2. Align the two 7″ × 10″ pillow backs onto pillow front, wrong sides facing, so pillow backs overlap in the middle and all outside edges match. Pin layers together.

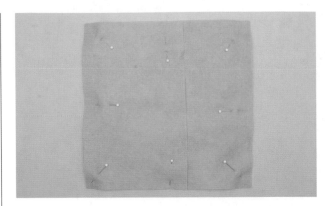

3. Flip pillow so front side is facing up. Again, sew all the way around the background fabric, this time keeping stitches very close to background edges.

4. Complete flange by sewing all around pillow, keeping close to outside edges. Insert 7″ pillow form through back opening.

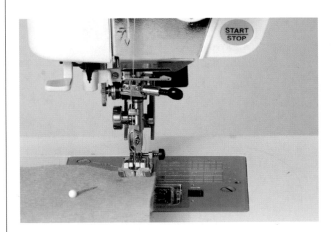

easy!

Create your own stencil by tracing simple shapes onto card stock and cutting them out.

Variations

A. Use letter stencils to create a personalized felted monogram appliqué that can be applied to a tote, jacket lapel, or journal cover.

B. You will notice that the other side of your needle felted design has an almost furry appearance. If you prefer, you might choose to have that side up.

stained glass
felting with yarn

NEEDLE FELTED BOOK TOTE

What You'll Need

- 1 rectangle 6˝ × 9˝ basil green felt for background
- 4 strips 1˝ × 18˝ basil green felt for straps
- 2 rectangles 9˝ × 12˝ blue felt for tote front and back panels
- Navy or black yarn for outline
- Roving in several colors, as shown, or your choice for fills (see color key on page 46)
- 1 rectangle 6˝ × 9˝ tulle, or nylon veiling

- Felting needle
- Foam pad
- Rotary cutter, ruler, and mat
- Markers, air soluble or chalk, and permanent
- Sewing machine and coordinating thread
- Optional: multineedle tool or embellisher machine

Here's a great design concept to jump-start your needle felting inspiration. Create your design by "drawing" a yarn outline onto your background. Then all you have to do is fill in each shape with needle felting, coloring book style, only much more sophisticated.

This jewel tone floral book tote showcases that style. Tuck in the latest best seller, and this would make a great bon voyage gift for a friend. Better make several though, because you'll want to keep one for yourself.

How-Tos
preparing design

Using a permanent marker, copy pattern template (page 46) onto tulle. Then, center tulle on background fabric, pin in place, and trace tulle pattern with air soluble or chalk marker. Remove tulle from background, and retrace to define lines, if necessary. Or sketch your own design on paper, and transfer it to the background fabric with tulle.

fun!
This design would make a glorious pillow.

beginning to felt

1. Place marked background fabric onto foam pad.

2. Needle felt yarn along traced pattern lines to create outlines. Continue needle felting until yarn is firmly attached to background fabric.

easy!

Skip marking the design, simply create a free-form pattern directly on the background fabric using yarn. Baste the yarn in place with a felting needle.

3. Place small amounts of roving inside outlined shapes, and begin needle felting, piercing along yarn edges and filling shapes completely.

4. Continue needle felting until all shapes have been filled and are firmly compacted.

fast!

For filling in large areas of color, use an embellisher machine.

5. Carefully remove background from foam. Trim with a rotary cutter and ruler to even up any distorted edges.

finishing touches

1. Make strap by pinning two 1˝ × 18˝ felt strips together, and then stitch close to edges all the way around outside edge. Repeat to make second strap.

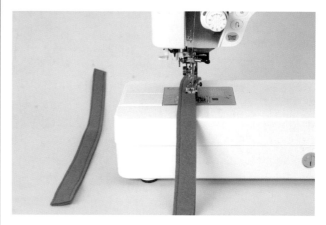

2. Position strap onto wrong side of tote front panel, and pin. Strap ends should extend 1½″ below top edge of front panel and be positioned 1½″ from each side. Sew across top edge of front panel. Repeat for back panel.

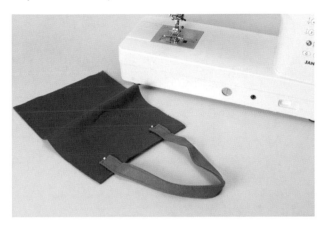

3. On back panel only, stitch around each strap end, forming a square as shown.

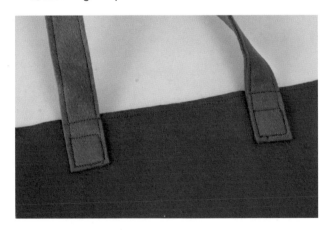

4. Center felted background in place on right side of front panel, and pin, being sure to catch strap ends when pinning. Sew around outer edges of background fabric, keeping stitches close to edge.

5. Align tote front and back panels, wrong sides facing, and carefully match edges. Sew down one side, across bottom, and up the other side, backstitching to secure.

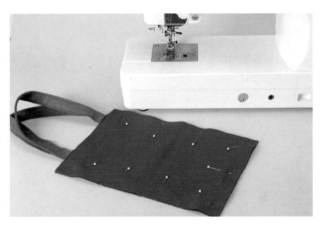

fun!

Create yarn outlines of holiday icons, and felt onto stockings, a table runner, or a tree skirt.

Variation

Instead of roving, use actual yarn to fill in all the shapes of an abstract design. The piece will end up looking a lot like embroidery.

painting with fiber,
color blending

NEEDLE FELTED PEAR STILL LIFE

Impress your friends with this project.

They'll never guess it was "felt by number."

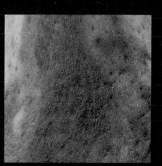

What You'll Need

- [ ] 10″ × 12″ rectangle felted wool for background
- [ ] Wool roving in shades of brown, green, yellow, cream, orange, cranberry, and purple (see color key on page 47)
- [ ] 1 rectangle 8″ × 10″ tulle, or nylon veiling
- [ ] Felting needle
- [ ] Foam pad
- [ ] Rotary cutter, ruler, and mat
- [ ] Markers, air soluble or chalk, and permanent
- [ ] Mounting board, precut mat with oval opening
- [ ] 1 sheet Supertape double-sided adhesive, 8½″ × 11″ (ThermoWeb, *see Resources*)
- [ ] Optional: multineedle tool or embellisher machine

Long before I was a needle felter, I was a painter, so the idea of blending colors and creating light and shade is near and dear to my heart. The infinite variety of luminous colors and sumptuous textures that wool roving imparts is a painter's dream come true.

This single pear appears to be as simple as a child's crayon drawing and yet on closer inspection reveals an intricate study of light, texture, and color. The luscious ripe fruit is depicted in a strong light with correspondingly strong shadows. Colored roving has been needle felted to the surface in thin layers, just as a painter would add pigment, blending slightly with the layers beneath to reveal rich and complex hues and tones.

How-Tos
preparing design

Using a permanent marker, copy pattern template (page 47) onto tulle. Then center tulle on felt background fabric, pin in place, and trace tulle pattern with air soluble or chalk marker. Remove tulle from background, and retrace to define lines, if necessary. Or sketch your own design on paper, and transfer it to the background fabric with tulle.

fun!

Work from a photograph of a flower, fruit, or vegetable for inspiration.

beginning to felt

1. Place background fabric onto foam pad. Begin needle felting the basic shapes in cream, yellow, and green roving, basting in place by piercing repeatedly with felting needle.

2. Add brown shapes for shadow and stem.

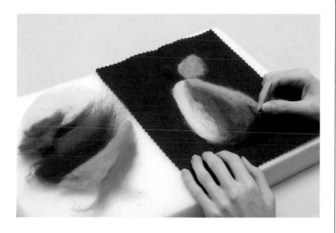

3. Spread roving into thin layers, and add high-lights and shadows, blemishes on the fruit, and so forth.

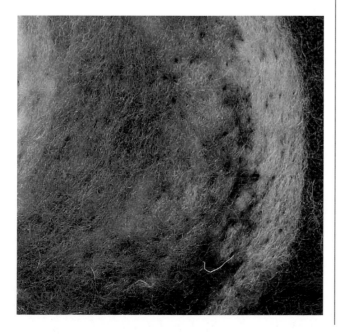

fast!

For filling in large areas of color, use an embellisher machine or multineedle tool.

4. Carefully remove background from foam. Trim any distorted edges with a rotary cutter and ruler.

finishing touches

Use double-sided adhesive to attach finished design to mounting board. Frame mounted project with a precut mat.

easy!

This design would make a glorious pillow. Simply start with a larger piece of fabric.

Variation

Choose a simple flower design from a gardening catalog, and create your own "felt by number" designs.

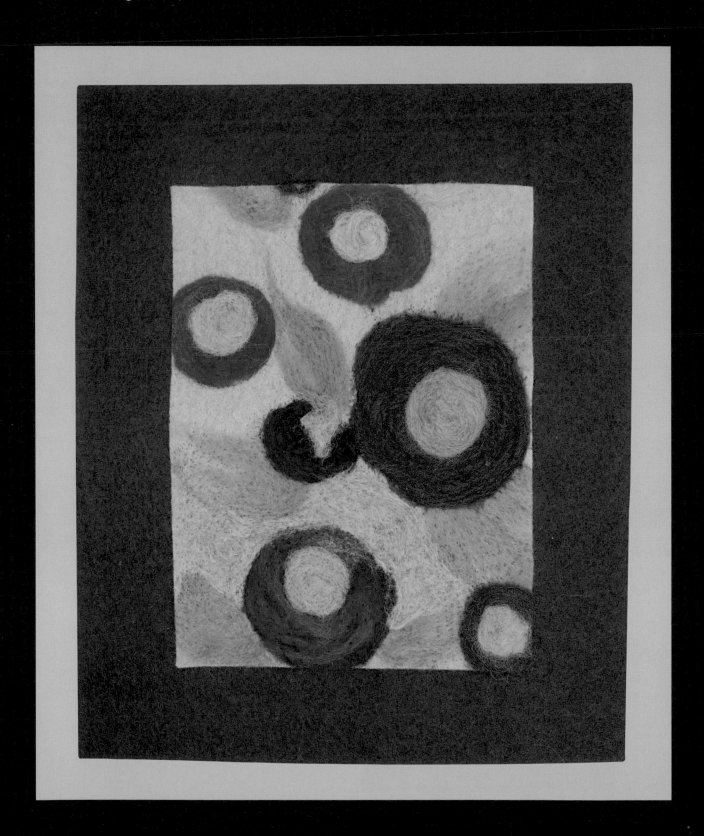

PATTERN TEMPLATES

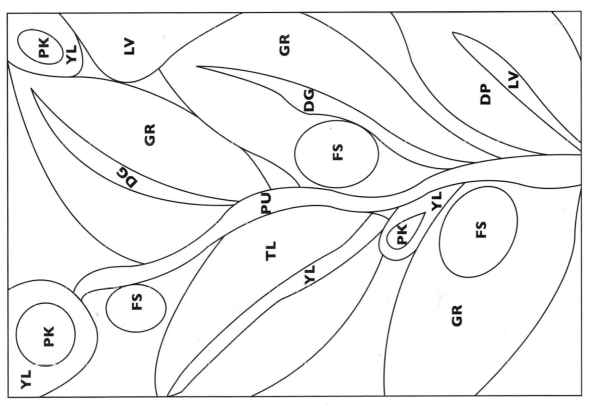

Mini-Seascape

BL=Blue

WH=White

YO=Yellow-Orange

YL=Yellow

Mosaic Journal Cover

GR=Green

DG=Dark Green

TL–Teal

PU=Purple

DP=Dark Purple

LV=Lavender

FS=Fuchsia

YL=Yellow

PK=Pink

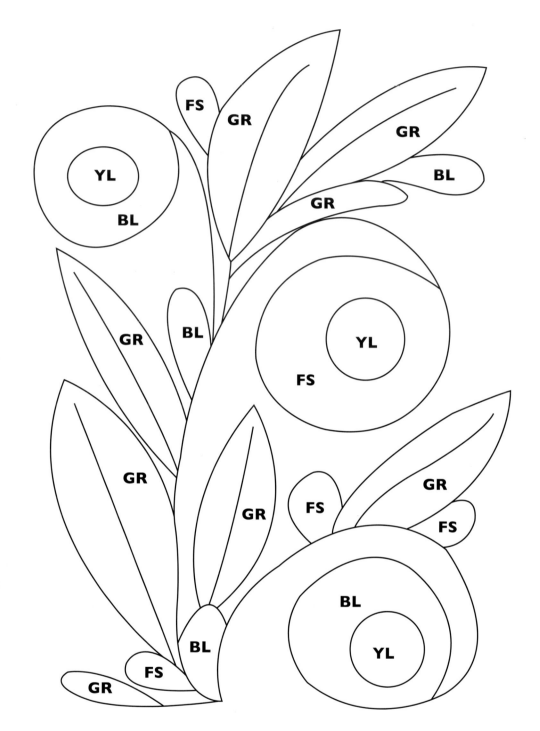

Book Tote

GR=Green

BL=Blue

FS=Fuchsia

YL=Yellow

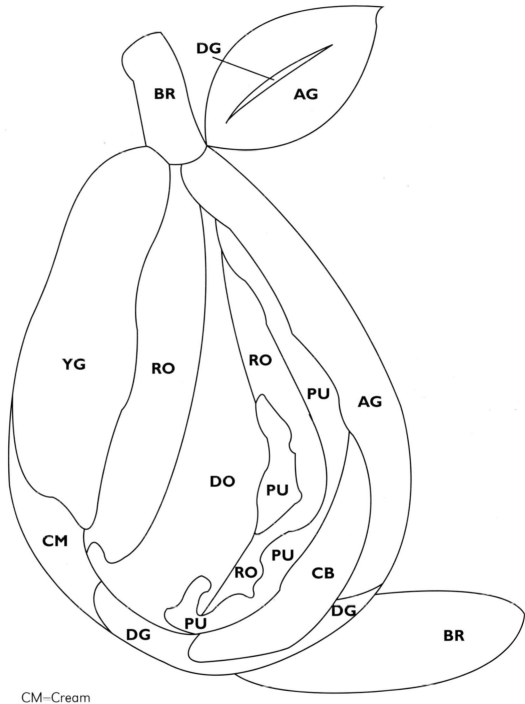

Pear Still Life

BR=Brown   CM=Cream

YG=Yellow-Green   RO=Red-Orange

AG=Apple Green   DO=Deep Orange-Rust

DG=Dark Green   PU=Purple

CB=Cranberry

About the Author

Photo by Sonny Knox

Lynne Farris brings a lifetime of experience in fabric arts to the world of crafts and do-it-yourself home décor. Her designs are often featured in leading craft magazines, and she is a frequent guest on HGTV. She works as a creative consultant to several leading manufacturers and is the owner of Lynne Farris Gallery in Atlanta, Georgia, where many of her textile works are on display. To learn more about Lynne, visit her website at www.lynnefarrisdesigns.com.

Resources

Lynne Farris Designs
1101 Juniper Street #404
Atlanta, GA 30309
www.lynnefarrisdesigns.com
Needle felting tools, kits, and supplies

Artgirlz
4537B Old Post Road
Charlestown, RI 02813
www.artgirlz.com
Charmz, feltz, and other fabulous stuff

Weeks Dye Works
1510-103 Mechanical Boulevard
Garner, NC 27529
877-OVERDYE
www.weeksdyeworks.com
Hand-dyed felted wools and fibers
(wholesale only)

Colonial Needle, Inc.
74 Westmoreland Avenue
White Plains, NY 10606
1-800-9 NEEDLE (800-963-3353)
www.colonialneedle.com
Felting needles and holders
(wholesale only)

Babylock Dealer Locator
www.babylock.com
embellisher machine

National Nonwovens
PO Box 150
Easthampton, MA 01027
www.nationalnonwovens.com
Wool felt and needle felting supplies
(wholesale only)

Ogier Trading Company
PO Box 686
Moss Beach, CA 94038
800-637-3207
Hand-dyed yarns and fibers
(wholesale only)

Plaid Simply Stencils
www.plaidonline.com
Available at major craft stores

ThermoWeb
Supertape double-sided adhesive
www.thermoweb.com
Available at major craft stores